My Child's
SEXUALITY

Frédérique Saint-Pierre
Marie-France Viau

My Child's
SEXUALITY

Éditions du
CHU Sainte-Justine

Bibliothèque et Archives nationales du Québec and Library and Archives Canada cataloguing in publication

Saint-Pierre, Frédérique, 1968-
    My child's sexuality
    (Questions/answers for parents)
    Translation of: Que savoir sur la sexualité de mon enfant?.
    ISBN 978-2-89619-149-9
        1. Children - Sexual behavior - Miscellanea. 2. Children and sex - Miscellanea. 3. Psychosexual development - Miscellanea. 4. Sex instruction for children - Miscellanea. I. Viau, Marie-France. II. Title.

    HQ784.S45S2313 2009   306.7083   C2008-942663-0

Graphic Design: Nicole Tétreault
Cover page and inside photos: Nancy Lessard

Éditions du CHU Sainte-Justine
3175, Côte-Sainte-Catherine
Montreal (Quebec) H3T 1C5
Telephone: (514) 345-4671 • Fax: (514) 345-4631
www.chu-sainte-justine.org/editions

    Legal Deposit: Bibliothèque et Archives nationales du Québec, 2009
                    Library and Archives Canada, 2009

The Sainte-Justine Hospital Foundation wishes to thank the generous donors who contributed to *UniverSanté des familles* and made it possible to create this new collection for families.
Thank you for your support... for the love of children!

Table of contents

Sexuality: the child's and the adult's

Psychosexual development

Sexuality: the child's and the adult's

▶ **What are the differences between children's sexuality and adult sexuality?**

Children's sexuality is different from that of adults in several ways, both physical and psychological. It is very important not to confuse our adult knowledge and experience of sex with what we observe, and think we know, about the sexuality of children.

First of all, children are physiologically immature and their genitals are not fully developed before puberty. Moreover, children are in a constant state of development and their sexuality, from one phase to another, is focussed on a number of sensitive zones of the body, not only the genitals. In psychosexual terms, the skin, mouth and anal area have great importance for children long before the genital region becomes a source of interest. Knowledge acquired earlier (at the oral and anal stages, for example) provides a basis from which children can move on to the next stage. Thus children's sexuality evolves as part of a general process of development and change.

Finally, it is important not to compare or confuse children's motivations with those of adults. Their relationship to sexuality is very different. Indeed, in children, sexuality underlies things like the need to know (curiosity), the quest for identity, pleasure and sensation, needs that evolve from one phase to the next in a child's development. Those needs are not of the same nature as adult sexuality, which is governed by the quest for genital pleasure, for example, or rituals of seduction and the desire for procreation.

To understand children, it is important to adopt their own outlook rather than view them through adult eyes. It is especially important that we do not project our own issues onto them.

Psychosexual development

▶ When and how does children's sexuality begin?

The sex of children is an issue even before they are born. From the moment the parents decide to have a child, the baby takes form in their minds. Throughout pregnancy, parents imagine the child and expectations start to form. In the great majority of cases, a child's sex matters a great deal, and the decision of whether or not to ask about it is a key issue for expectant parents. It is natural to form images of the child, based on projections and desires, even before he or she is born. Meanwhile, the people around the future parents make predictions (sometimes accurate, sometimes not), and tests such as ultrasound or amniocentesis make it possible to find out a baby's sex before birth. Some parents want to know as soon as possible whereas others prefer to be surprised, thus preserving their mental image of the baby a little longer.

Did you know?
It is estimated that 70 to 80% of future parents ask to know their baby's sex ahead of time. They ask most of all for a first child whereas with the second, they prefer to be surprised.

A child's sex greatly influences the attitudes and choices made by parents and other adults around them. All of these people have their own relationship to sex and to other men and women – parents, brothers and sisters, friends or lovers. Obviously, a baby's sex influences the style and colour of their clothes, nursery decor and toys, affectionate nicknames they are given and ways of interacting with them, as well as people's expectations, hopes and fears on their behalf.

Naturally babies have no idea whether they are girls or boys; it is the people around them to whom it matters. Children are born male or female, biologically, but not masculine or feminine – and certainly not "men" or "women"! They must go through several stages of separation, individuation and identification before developing a sense of themselves as sexual beings. It takes several years for children to become fully aware of their own gender.

▶ Why do babies put everything in their mouths?

Sucking is a basic reflex, a movement babies can make from the 16th week of gestation. Ultrasounds reveal that even before birth, the foetus often sucks its thumb. This sucking, or suckling, reflex is essential to babies' survival, for without it they would not be able to take in nourishment.

Though the act of sucking is closely linked to the need for nourishment and relief from hunger, children also derive pleasure from non-nutritive sucking, which stimulates the mouth. Through sucking their thumb, a pacifier, their security blanket or the ear of teddy bear, babies keep themselves occupied and calm. It is the first pleasure that babies give themselves, an auto-erotic satisfaction.

Approximately 80% of children under 2 suck one of their fingers, especially after they are weaned from the breast or bottle, so as to re-experience this sensation of pleasure.

The sucking of the thumb, pacifier or other objects is the most striking expression of the oral stage, which children go through between 0 and 15 months. During this time, the mouth is the main erogenous zone and source of pleasurable sensation. It is also via the mouth that children explore the world. During the oral stage, babies put unknown objects in their mouths and thus become acquainted with the world around them. Through their mouths they discover objects (their rattle, their stuffed toy), their own bodies (their fists, their toes) and those of their parents (Mommy's nose, Daddy's chin).

Did you know?

It is only around the age of 3 that children can tell the difference between male and female, and which sex they themselves belong to. They become capable of correctly answering questions such as: "Are you a boy or a girl?" "Are you like this doll (boy) or this one (girl)?" "When you grow up, will you be a daddy or a mommy?" Around the age of 5 or 6, children acquire the notion of gender constancy ("I will always be a girl" or "I will always be a boy").

▶ **Should I breast feed or bottle feed?**

The decision of whether to breast or bottle feed comes down to the mother, though the subject may be discussed by both parents. The benefits of breastfeeding, for both mother and baby, have long been recognized. Breast-feeding (or nursing) provides a rare kind of intimacy and shared pleasure for both mother and child. Still, some women are not comfortable with nursing. They cannot accept the idea that their relationship with their child will involve the meeting of baby's body with mother's breasts. Sometimes, too, insurmountable problems arise in breast-feeding. When nursing is problematic, infants are better off being bottle-fed by a calm and relaxed mother than breast-fed by a mother who is tense and ambivalent.

▶ **Are there disadvantages to breast-feeding?**

Yes, sometimes with older children, that is, in the case of prolonged nursing, the mother's body may become a source of overstimulation for the children, rather than nourishment and affectionate contact. There comes a time when they must be able to grow away from the mother's body and understand that they can touch and handle it as they please.

▶ **Should I give my baby a pacifier?**
What if he keeps asking for it when he's older?

Should we give newborns pacifiers? Opinions are divided and advocates for both sides can be quite vocal. There are advantages and disadvantages, and it is not easy to know which option to choose. The most common parental fears are that babies will develop a "dependency" on the pacifier or end up with dental malformations. Thumb-sucking, too, can interfere with good dental development, but it is rare for children to suck their thumb beyond a certain age. However, unlike a thumb, a pacifier must be sucked quite hard to keep it in the mouth and is often dirty from having repeatedly fallen out. Most of all, the pacifier is too often an easy way out, a way of making children instantly "behave": a few tears and presto! in goes the pacifier to plug the hole! But in the end, whether you are for or against the use of pacifiers, it must be acknowledged that some babies like sucking and their need to do so goes beyond nutritive sucking or the desire to explore new objects with the mouth.

Though we still do not know much about the physio-logical origins of sucking and its soothing effect, it is clear from observing babies that through sucking they are able to keep themselves calm, for example when they are strapped into their car-seat or their parents are not available.

However, when children over 2 continue to suck their thumb or ask for the pacifier on a daily basis, it can become a going concern for parents. In an effort to keep children in a good mood, they may find that they have become slaves to the pacifier! This can become a major issue in the parent-child relationship. Some shy, emotional and anxious children continue sucking to calm themselves and ease stress-related tension. However, it is important to make a distinction between short periods of regression due to circumstantial insecurity (the birth of a new baby, a separation from a parent, a major change in daily routine) and a more sustained form of anxiety.

If we become overwhelmed by the daily trials of "pacifier management," it is important to identify possible sources of anxiety in children's lives. For indeed, the child's need for the pacifier is a symptomatic behaviour. Besides taking direct action to deal with stress-producing factors in children's lives, it is also a good idea to introduce a "transitional object" to replace the pacifier. By providing children with a concrete means of support, you can limit the use of the pacifier to the private space of bedroom and bed. It is also a good idea to talk to children, reassure them with words and images, because their ability to create mental pictures goes hand-in-hand with their ability to regulate their emotions more independently.

▶ **Why is my child's "blankie" so important to him?**

Towards the end of the first year and the beginning of the second, children often become attached to a special object, which they choose themselves and which becomes very important to them. It may be a blanket, a stuffed toy or even a scrap of fabric that children handle sensually, suck or rub against their nose, or stroke between two fingers. They drag it around everywhere - and yet it always disappears just at the moment when it is most needed! Children are more attached to this object than to anything else, and this can last for years. "Blankie" or "Teddy" can withstand anything: passionate caresses, aggressive biting, tears and runny noses.

Gradually the object becomes permeated with familiar smells – a little of Mommy's, a little of Daddy's, and maybe the dog's too! When children inhale these odours, they picture their loved ones, or places where they feel happy and secure. These images reassure and soothe them, give them a sense of being safe and not alone. In short, the transitional object helps children endure the sorrow they feel when Mommy goes away; it helps them transform an empty, waiting time into a quiet relaxed time filled with daydreams.

▶ **Why is the toilet-training stage such a challenge for children and their parents?**

From 15 months to 2 ½ years, when children learn to walk and their language develops, the anal zone becomes a focal point for sensation and for certain parent-child issues as well. At this age, children are becoming more independent and physiologically adept at controlling their sphincters. Parents can expect a new period to begin. They no longer have to change diapers, but on the other hand they are faced with the task of negotiating with a small child who is learning how to exert control over his body (letting himself go or holding back, giving pleasure to himself or to Mommy and Daddy), over his desires and emotions, and most of all, his parents.

This is an intense and tumultuous period when children make many discoveries and conquests. It becomes obvious that they must learn to compromise with the increasingly specific demands of their parents. What will they agree to? What will they not want to do? Physiologically, children experience the alternation of tension and relaxation that is the basis of pleasure. Moreover, they become aware of the effect this has on the people around them. What parent has never exclaimed: "Oh, what a nice big poop! What a big boy/girl you are!" Between parents and children a new dynamic is established. Now children, with their own bodies, are producing a kind of offering for the parents, who in turn often receive it as if it were a gift – though one that is much more welcome when it arrives at the right time and place!

The question that faces children is this: to give the "gift" at the right time and place (in the potty or toilet), thus submitting to the parents' desires, or not submitting and letting go anywhere (usually in their pants, when they are zipped into their snowsuit), or, then again, holding back and worrying Mommy ("He hasn't gone potty for two days now!"). Sphincter control gives children a certain amount of parent control as well! How sad parents look when Baby has gone in his diaper, but how proud they are when he goes in the potty! At such times, children feel they are all-powerful: I'm the one who decides to submit or revolt!

This is also one of the first times in their lives that children are asked to take care of themselves. When children are sufficiently mature physiologically to control their sphincters, they can wilfully let themselves go or hold back. This is when psychoaffective maturity starts to develop. Generally, we become aware that the process has begun when children start letting parents know when their diaper needs changing, and later by indicating when they are about to eliminate. They also show interest in other people's trips to the bathroom, needing to see what they leave in the toilet and watch it disappear with the flush. All children are interested in what they leave in their potty. That is how they make the distinction between inside and out, and it fascinates them.

Sometimes they also want to examine and touch what they have just expelled. Some children even experience anxiety seeing a part of themselves whirled away with a rush of water. They see the toilet as a bottomless hole into which they too are in danger of falling and being flushed away, if they make a wrong move.

▶ Until what age can children sleep in our bed? How do we make them leave once they've got used to sleeping there?

There are many different circumstances that may bring children to sleep in their parents' bed. Some children go to sleep with their parents for reassurance when it is thundering outside, or when they have had a nightmare. Sometimes parents allow their children into bed with them in the very early morning. There are children who fall asleep at night in their parents' bed and are carried to their own beds. Then there are more complicated situations in which children more or less take up residence in the parents' bed. This happens sometimes with children who sleep with one parent while the other is working, or when the parents are separated. It is also the case with anxious children who want to avoid the moment of solitude before sleep by cuddling up to someone.

When this kind of behaviour arises, it is important for parents to be aware of what is stopping them (often unconsciously) from warmly but firmly taking children back to their own beds. Indeed, like some children, some parents dread solitude and appreciate the comforting presence of their children. Or maybe the parents find it difficult to be alone together in bed. Certainly, it must be remembered that small boys and girls are not spouses and must not get into the habit of sleeping in the parents' bed when mother or father is out or gone away. Children cannot, and must not, replace wives or husbands. They are not adults and must not be expected to reassure an anxious or lonely parent. If they are asked to do so, the intergenerational barrier breaks down, which makes children anxious. Moreover, when this kind of situation persists, it can awaken precocious sexual urges in children. Parents who are personally dealing with an emotionally painful situation and are ignorant of how their behaviour affects their children, may find it difficult to reverse the situation. Once children have made a place for themselves in the big bed, they are not going to leave without a fight!

Did you know?

Some words are funnier than others! Small children use with pleasure and feverish excitement words such as "peepee", "poop", "bum", "fart". Children assert themselves by using these "bad" words, grownup words. They say them out of enjoyment but also to test the reactions of adults. The more you react to these words, the more children will say them. However, they end up getting bored with the game, especially if you do not pay too much attention. If you cannot resist saying something, simply explain that these are words we do not say in public, but in the privacy of the bedroom or even better, the bathroom, where such words originated!

Before they can correct the situation, parents must be ready to identify the "payoff" they are getting from this kind of closeness with their children, and agree to give it up. If this is your case, you may need a little help from someone you can confide in. When it comes time to explain to children why they have to sleep in their own bed (e.g.: "you're a big boy/girl now"; "Mommy wants to sleep alone"; "Mommy and Daddy want to sleep together"), children must be reassured that the parent or parents are in the house watching over them and are ready to offer comfort if they are afraid of the dark or of monsters.

Reassuring compromises must be made (a night-light, a magic monster-fighting teddy bear, keeping the door open a crack...). It is important to establish a bedtime routine: teeth brushing, a goodnight kiss, then lights out. This routine will prepare children for sleep one stage at a time, so they will not be taken by surprise. Finally, it is important to create moments of pleasure before and after sleep so that it becomes a special time. Before children go to bed, tell them a story as they sit cuddled warmly next to Mommy or Daddy, and in the morning, you can all meet again in the parents' bed after everyone has had a good sleep.

▶ Why do little girls want to be Daddy's princess and boys want to be Mommy's little man?

Between the ages of 3 and 5, children express a desire to be closer to the opposite-sex parent and feel a certain rivalry with the same-sex parent. It is during this Oedipal period that children first assert their gender; their sexual identity becomes consolidated and the foundation is laid for their future course as adults in love. During this period, despite their young age, children come to understand two important principles: the difference between the sexes (boys and girls) and between the generations (adults and children). This understanding helps structure their own self-representation in their relations with others. Boys with their mothers, and daughters with their fathers establish complementary relationships with a desire for recognition and exclusive love. This time of delicious illusions mixed with bitter disillusionment is a very constructive period in children's lives. They discover the possibility of defining themselves more clearly as boys or girls. And, through the parents' refusal to allow children's fantasies to become reality, they also learn that certain taboos exist and cannot be broken.

Did you know?

Songs and games in which parts of the body are named e.g. "Head, shoulder knees and toes [...] Eyes and ears and mouth and nose" (etc.) help children enlarge their vocabulary and develop a mental picture of their own body. In a similar way, using the correct terms for the parts of the body, including the genital organs, helps put children at ease with their bodies.

The boy, his Mommy and... Daddy

A baby boy's first close relationship is with his mother's body. It is also with Mother that his Oedipal complex is played out during his third year, in other words quite early. It is important to recognize how having a son and being close to him is a source of pride for a mother. Baby boy in his mother's arms, reflected in her eyes, is Mommy's little man!

Around the age of 3, the boy clearly expresses his desire to be close to his mother and enjoy her exclusive love. He is affectionate and seeks his mother's displays of affection. They make him feel proud, both in private and in front of his father, whom he feels he is dominating, if only for a moment. This is a time of naive but heartfelt declarations: "When I grow up, I'm going to marry you!" The little boy needs to be made to feel welcome as he builds himself up as a little man, with Mommy showing her affection and Daddy authorizing this close relationship. But it is all a question of degree, and Daddy must also remain the biggest and strongest, the one who gets to be intimate with Mommy because she is his wife. And, after years of attachment to his first love object, the boy will need his father's help to free himself from his attachment to his mother.

The girl, her Mommy, her Daddy and... her Mommy

For little girls too, the first intimate contact is with their mother's bodies. However, whereas boys remain attached to their mothers from birth to the end of the Oedipal period, girls must pull away earlier to transfer their affections to their fathers. This is an important difference in the development of girls and boys. And this early detachment from the mother is not easy, either for Mommy or the little girl. Another distinction to be made between the mother-son and mother-daughter relationship is that because they are the same sex, the baby girl is like a mirror for her mother. Often when mothers look at their baby daughters, it is partly themselves they are seeing. And during the Oedipal period, when the girl confronts her mother to make a place for herself in her father's heart, this mirror effect sometimes confuses issues.

Around the age of 3, when a girl seeks the love and attention of her father, she turns away from her mother. She may, in fact, consider herself quite different from her mother; and indeed, by identifying the ways in which she differs from her mother, the girl will establish her own identity. That way, once she leaves Oedipus behind and starts to identify with her mother again, she will see herself both as "a girl like Mommy" but also a girl with her own distinct personality. Little girls, like little boys, need to feel welcomed by their father and viewed with affectionate admiration. Mommy can play along by trying to avoid getting in the way without good reason. Still, it is important for her to give the girl a "reality check" from time to time in order to protect Daughter from her own desires, which can end up causing her anxiety. The little girl must understand that Daddy loves her very much but will never be her lover or husband.

▶ How does parental separation affect children during the Oedipal period?

Parental separation, when young children are involved, can present certain pitfalls. When the separation occurs at the height of the Oedipal period and a father leaves behind not only his spouse but also his little girl (or vice-versa, a mother leaves the father and son), children suffer true heartbreak. They are losing their complementary relationship and the parent whose admiration they seek. This means that the children themselves, as little men and women, are being called into question and may feel inadequate. It is important to make children understand that it is two grownup people who are separating, not parents from children, and try to foster a close relationship between mother and son and father and daughter.

Furthermore, a separation leaves an empty place in the home, a place once occupied by the departed mother or father. There is a player missing in the Oedipal drama and children are left with too much space to fill. It is up to parents, if there is no boyfriend or girlfriend on the scene, to make children understand that excessive closeness cannot be allowed. Even if parents remain single, the prospect of a boyfriend or girlfriend remains present as a potential, both in their minds and the children's.

Separated parents must learn to avoid denigrating their estranged spouse in front of the children. Children need an opposite-sex parent as a rival during the Oedipal period, as well as a model with which to identify when leaving this phase of their development. This process of identification can become very disrupted if Mommy (or Daddy) paints a negative portrait of his or her "ex." In such conditions, how could a little girl want to become "a woman like Mommy", or a little boy "a man like Daddy"?

▶ Why is it "boys with boys and girls with girls" when children are 6-12 years?

Between the ages of 6 and 12, children like to spend time with others of their own gender: boys with boys and girls with girls. They recognize and identify with each other, and protect themselves from games of seduction. In their dealings with the opposite sex, some even display a rather chauvinistic attitude: boys are better than girls, or vice-versa. The point of it all is to prove to others and themselves that they are "real" boys or "real" girls.

Contact with the opposite sex can also be a subject of mockery within a group. Does this mean these children are totally uninterested in the opposite sex? As a matter of fact, no, but their interest is expressed in a contrary, antagonistic fashion – girls criticizing boys and vice-versa. Their perception of what it is to be a man or a woman is often quite stereotyped and lacking in finer details. This has to do with children's need for clear reference points concerning gender to minimize any possible ambiguity between masculine and feminine.

During this period, children need heroes and role models, usually ones of their own sex. These models help compensate for their feelings of powerlessness in the adult world. When they are younger, children choose their heroes in their family; Daddy or Mommy, big brother or big sister. Now they turn to their companions, and choose the one everyone loves and admires, or the one who does things that no one else would dare to do.

Admiration also plays an important role in children's relationship with their best friend, a close and tender bond. Think of two or three boys planning a trick or an adventure together; or of girls who hug each other affectionately when they meet each morning in the schoolyard. Of course, these special friendships often change, they form and fall apart. However some last for a long time, in enduring fidelity.

Did you know?

Children of primary school age are often very shy about sex, going so far as to call anything to do with sex "disgusting". This does not mean they are not interested in sex; they are simply poking fun at what makes them feel uncomfortable. That way they can talk about the subject without really talking about it, camouflaging their curiosity.

▶ My child is "in love." What am I to think and say?

Many parents are very surprised to discover or learn that their child is in love. This occurs at the height of a period when children shyly pass each other love notes in class, or ask a friend to deliver them. We witness the formation of short-lived couples based on attractions that have little to do with the kind that draw teenage or adult couples together. However, it is a kind of preparation for what will happen later. Parents sometimes fear seeing their children become involved so young in a "romantic relationship." They fear that their little one might be hurt or engage in sexual games.

First we should examine what it means for children to be in love. Why not ask your son or daughter what they see in the other person, and what they do when they are together? In general, these childhood lovers want most of all to play and laugh together, share activities they both enjoy. But they may also be motivated by a need for attention or a fear of being alone. The discovery that their child is in love is also, for parents, a golden opportunity to talk to him or her about feelings, respect, and what one can find in a special relationship with another person. And though they may seem naive, children's feelings of love are sincere. Their disappointments and heartbreaks are often experienced with an intensity that must not be underestimated.

How to react if your child is in love? To begin with, count yourself lucky that he or she told you about it, for these are very precious secrets. Listen to your child without diminishing or exaggerating the situation. Most of all, do not laugh, mock or tease your child, in private or in public. And if your child does not want to talk about it, respect these wishes but remain on the lookout for signs of uneasiness or sadness.

▶ Why are pre-teens so concerned with their image?

The bodies of pre-teens transform, but all the parts don't grow at the same time, temporarily creating an impression of physical disproportion and imbalance. Sometimes young people wonder if their bodies, including their sex organs, are normal. They inevitably compare themselves to friends whose pace of development is different from their own. Everything about their bodies is subject to comparison: noses, height, weight and even penises or breasts.

Furthermore, the anxiety caused by this strange new body makes young people highly sensitive to the remarks of others. Pre-teens and teens are extremely aware of their bodies as seen through the eyes of others. Girls may be proud of their new breasts, but also shy and ashamed about being more visibly sexual than other girls. They certainly do not need anyone to comment on their breasts, for example to exclaim teasingly: "Look, look, they're getting bigger!" As for boys, their voices start to change and they often utter discordant sounds that they would rather no one noticed.

The issues surrounding these transformations are very sensitive because young people's body-image can be distorted by what they think other people see, and by their own idea of what is socially acceptable or desirable. For this reason, advertising has a great impact on them. Their body-image is conditioned by a combination of hopes, fears and complexes.

Pre-teens ask themselves many questions such as: how can I feel good about a body that is changing? How will I ever learn to like myself? How do I approach other people? To feel comfortable in this changing body, young people must first understand what is happening to them. They must realize that they are going through a period of great changes, both physical and psychological, and that it will take a certain time, and that everyone develops at their own rhythm. Young people should be encouraged to acknowledge the parts of their bodies that they like – the ones they think are fine the way they are. Parents should highlight the value of their personality, for it plays a major role in forming relationships with others.

Physical modesty, privacy

▶ When does physical modesty first appear in children?

From the age of 5 or 6, then during the latency period (approximately 6 to 8 years), children display a growing need for privacy in their family sphere. They are embarrassed by any mention of sex and there is a change in their attitude to nudity. They start closing the door of the bathroom and bedroom, will not change clothes in front of others, etc.

For some children, displays of affection also become a source of embarrassment. From now on, parents must be content with verbal, rather than physical expressions of tenderness and other feelings. Children make it clear that there is no more need for touching and certainly no need for kisses from Mommy in front of their friends! This is also an age when kissing on the mouth, a normal gesture in some families, can change its meaning for young people, become sexually charged, so must be avoided.

It is important to respect children's new physical modesty. One must not make fun of it, laugh about it or point it out in public, because it exposes children to the eyes of others when all they want is to be alone and have their privacy respected. At this stage of their lives, they are building their own territory, a little at a time.

Children also develop a need for privacy about feelings; secret thoughts are confided to a diary, notes are exchanged between friends. Children gradually acquire their own way of thinking; they keep some of their thoughts secret and confide others to people close to them. In this way they assert themselves as distinct beings.

▶ When should I stop taking baths with my child?

It is quite common for family members to share a bath, parents with children or brothers and sisters together. This practice is economical both in terms of time and energy, as well as pleasant and fun, but it eventually comes to an end. It would be quite surprising to see a teenager share a bath with a parent or sibling. Most of the time, the end comes without anyone having to think about it. Parents no longer offer, children no longer ask.

Did you know?

Children need privacy from a very young age. Physical modesty is learned through daily gestures, such as bathing, grooming, rituals of hygiene, and getting ready for bed. It is also developed through affectionate contact and the family's respect for a special place the child cherishes, either real and concrete (a place in the house that "belongs" to the child) or symbolic (allowing a child time alone to think). Through this learning process, children define their space, and by doing so, define themselves in relation to others. By showing their respect for children's need for privacy, parents help them learn how to assert this need and have it respected by others in the future.

Parents should adapt to children's development. With a baby or young children, who in the bath-tub are fully occupied in playing with bubbles or bath toys, the attention is rarely focussed on the other's nudity - or at least, only long enough for children to want to touch the other's sexual parts, such as mother's breasts. In this sense, bath-time provides a good opportunity for parents to find out what children want to know, and calmly explain that, for example, a breast is not a toy but a part of Mommy's body that children cannot touch whenever they feel like it. In the latency period, the communal bath becomes less of an issue, especially when it comes to the combinations of father-daughter, mother-son, or brother-sister. In any case, certain rituals of grooming and hygiene are no longer performed by parents, because children have become sufficiently independent to do them alone. If parents insist on continuing to do them, children will feel very uncomfortable.

Whatever children's age, we must be attentive to their need for privacy and feelings of physical modesty. They may not express them in words but in little changes in attitude. When their own nudity or that of others becomes disturbing or over-exciting, it is best for parents to create boundaries and let everyone have their own space.

▶ My child likes to be naked; should I allow this?

Around the age of 3, children cease to be indifferent to their own nudity or that of others. They even like it. They find it amusing to show themselves off, and see how nice they look in their "birthday suit", as reflected in the eyes of their parents. They like running around the house naked when they get out of the bath, they can even go so far as to attract attention to their private parts (look at my bum, look at my penis), most of the time with a certain feverish excitement. There are circumstances in which this behaviour is appropriate, or at least without consequences; for example, when children are very young and the behaviour is limited to the privacy of the home. Sometimes, though, it is less appropriate and can make people uneasy. In that case, it is best to intervene and ask children to get dressed because their behaviour is making others feel uncomfortable.

Did you know?

When children ask questions about sex, we are well advised to let them talk for a while before we answer. We might ask them: "What do you think about that?", "Why do you want to know?" By drawing children out in this way, we are better equipped to evaluate their level of knowledge and adapt our information to what they already know and want to know. For example, children of 4 might want to know how babies are made; and they are ready to hear about Daddy's little seed and the egg in Mommy's stomach, but do not want to know how the seed gets to the egg and in fact, do not need to know.

▶ **Can we be naked around our children?**

Attitudes towards nudity vary greatly from one family to the next, depending on background, family values and the parents' upbringing. However, one thing is sure: there should be no ambiguity about it, that is, adults' behaviour must be devoid of all sexual connotation. Even when the situation seems clear for adults, it is not always quite as clear for children. Indeed, from the age of 2, bodily closeness can excite children, even when adults believe their own attitudes to be non-sexual. Thus it is important to establish certain boundaries between your body and theirs. These boundaries allow you to avoid contact that might seem ambiguous from your own point of view, and especially your child's point of view.

Caresses, hugs and kisses will obviously continue, but it must be made clear that these are simple shows of affection. Later, between the ages of 5 and 12, when children become more physically modest and are embarrassed by nudity (their own or that of others), parents must try to understand and respect this new reserve. They must adapt their conduct accordingly, while protecting their child's sensitivity.

▶ **What do we do if our child walks
in on us having sex?**

Some parents are afraid their child will discover them having sex and be traumatized. Obviously, you make an effort to prevent this from happening, but if it does happen, do not panic: it is not a catastrophe. Stay calm; avoid sending children away quickly in a climate of anxiety, as if they had committed a crime. If you sense that children are worried, reassure them and answer their questions. They may have heard noises that made them curious or frightened them.

Children can perceive the sex act as an act of aggression; they may think that one parent is hurting the other. It is important to make it clear to them that no one was hurting anyone, that these gestures were hugs and caresses that big people give each other when they love each other. You can tell them that these caresses are pleasant to give and to receive, but they are very private, between parents. That is why, you may explain, when the bedroom door is closed, you have to knock before entering.

Homosexuality

▶ Should I talk to my child about homosexuality?

School-aged children have generally heard people talk
about homosexuality, if not at home then in the schoolyard
or on television. They may have heard people use expressions, often pejorative (fag, faggot, homo), or seen media
images, which are often stereotypes. In any case, the information children are exposed to leaves something to be desired.
When broaching the subject of homosexuality with children,
we should talk about tolerance, acceptance and respect for
difference. That way you can fight prejudice.

If children ask "what does it mean to be gay?" we can
tell them that sometimes two people of the same sex fall
in love with each other and form a couple. Like all people
who love each other, they hug and kiss, and sometimes
choose to live together.

▶ Could my child be, or become homosexual?

Boys and girls form fundamental bonds within their
own gender, from early childhood through latency and
adolescence. Here we may cite the examples of father-son
or mother-daughter relationships in the post-Oedipal
identification phase; we may also think of the close bonds
that unite groups of boys or girls during latency, and the
unique "best friend" relationships of the teen years.
These alliances play an essential role in the development
of sexual identity. It must be emphasized that they do not
foreshadow a future homosexual orientation.

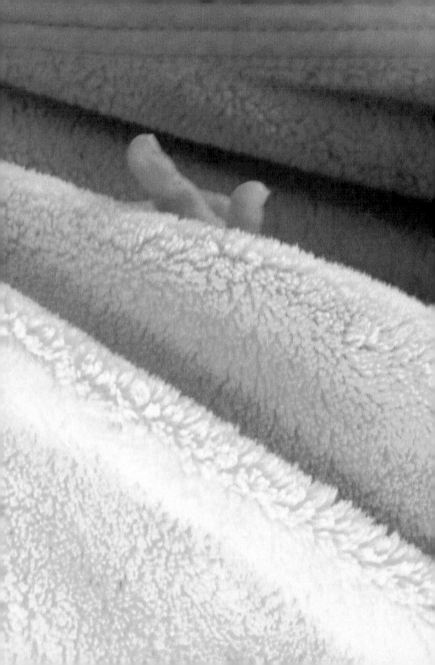

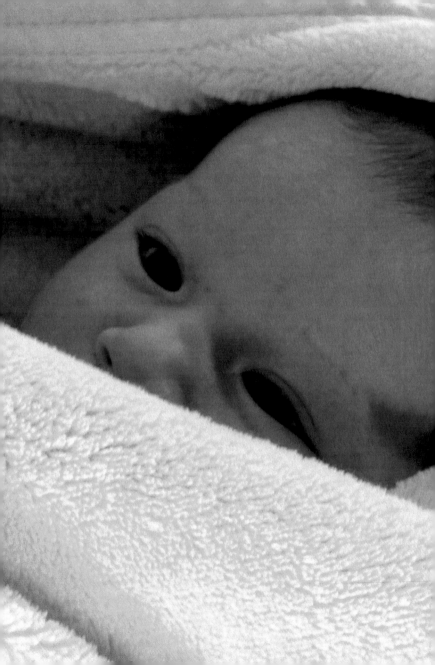

However, some children, from the pre-teen period through adolescence, experience doubts about their sexual orientation. They may, for a time, have homosexual or bisexual relationships and experiences. However, even if between the ages of 9 and 12, a young person fantasizes about, or is attracted to a person of the same sex, this is no definite indicator of his or her sexual orientation. Both girls and boys can be persuaded by friends to engage in homosexual activities, or feel the need to compare themselves to a person of the same sex to make sure they are physically normal. These are often simple explorations, ways of satisfying curiosity or relieving anxiety, rather than expressions of homosexual desire or orientation. However, some young people remain troubled about these experiences. They feel guilt and fear about having opened the door to this sort of questioning of their own sexual identity.

The homosexual identity

When we speak of "structural homosexuality" we are referring to individuals who, from an early age, are attracted by children of the same sex without at the same time rejecting their own biological gender. This tendency occurs naturally and children can do nothing to alter it. It is simply a fact, part of who they are -- not a question of will. Major studies on the subject estimate that 10% of the population is homosexual.

The question of sexual orientation, which takes root in childhood, is at the heart of identity. Homosexual male teens claim they felt different from other boys from the age of 5 or 6, without having made the connection between this feeling and their sexual orientation. As for adult homosexuals, they recall their first homosexual attractions as occurring around the age of 8 or 9. On average, it is around the age of 13 that homosexual men and women make the connection between their sense of being different and their sexual orientation, as expressed through their attractions to individuals of their own gender.

Around the age of 8 or 9, before the question of sexual orientation arises, some boys feel different from their companions in the sense that they have "feminine" interests, whereas some girls are interested in traditionally masculine activities. These "tomboy" or "effeminate" attitudes are generally quite striking and affect children's social integration even before the pre-teen years. While we are on this subject, we may point out that it is probably more difficult for boys with a feminine identity to be accepted by their peers than for "tomboy" girls, whose competition with boys is often viewed in a positive light as proof of "ambition." Due to more marked prejudices concerning male homosexuality, little boys with effeminate mannerisms are quickly identified and taunted with derogatory epithets (fag, faggot, homo).

In the pre-teen years, when erotic attraction becomes more conscious and fantasy life more active, the orientation of one's desires becomes clearer and can give rise to anxiety in some young people.

How should we react to our child's homosexuality?

Most parents react when they notice their child has "homosexual tendencies", though some do not see it as a serious problem. However, others are overwhelmed by negative or mixed emotions such as anger, shame and anxiety, and are uncertain about how to react.

Parents for whom homosexuality is "taboo" sometimes react inappropriately, causing great upheaval in their relationship with their child. These parents experience guilt and shame, considering their child's homosexuality as a sign of their own failure. Some fathers in particular react very negatively, feeling their virility has been called into question. Situations of conflict often result and bring about painful separations between parents and children. For this reason, young people, who in general greatly fear being rejected by people they love, tend to keep this part of themselves secret.

The discovery of homosexuality and its rejection, by parents and friends and the young people themselves, can lead to great distress and even suicidal behaviour. A Canadian study conducted by Bagley and Tremblay revealed that the rate of suicide attempts among young homosexuals is up to 13 times higher than among young heterosexuals.

Parents and other people in children's social environment must not view them only in terms of their sexuality. Instead, children must be seen for everything that they are, with all their personal characteristics taken into account. However, if a young person begins to use some aspect of his or her sexuality to provoke, manipulate and disturb others, in the aim of communicating unhappiness or anger, parents must set firm boundaries while keeping the door to communication open, in a spirit of mutual respect.

Health and physical development

▶ **My little girl has redness around her vulva.
Why is this, and what can I do to prevent it?**

This redness or itchiness of the vulva, without discharge, is called "vulvitis." The causes are natural or the result of external irritants, rather than infection or skin disease. One of the natural causes in very young girls is that the outer lips of the vagina (labia majora) have become too small to completely protect the vaginal mucous membranes. Moreover, after the age of 2 or 3, the levels of oestrogen transmitted by the mother during pregnancy have dropped, causing the mucous membranes of the girl's vagina to grow thinner, making them more susceptible to irritation. Finally, because the anus is very close to the vulva, irritation and even infection can result if girls do not wipe themselves properly after bowel movements.

External irritants such as perfumed soap, fabric softener, detergent, bubble bath, baby powder and shampoo can also cause the redness. Sometimes the vulva is irritated by underwear that is too tight or made from a fabric other than cotton, or by bathing suit bottoms, diapers or underwear that have remained wet or soiled for an extended period.

Most irritation of the vulva will disappear if you apply the following measures in your little girl's hygiene:

- to soothe discomfort, give her a plain bath (of about 15 minutes), with water only;

- daily baths rather than showers (this allows the natural vaginal secretions to soften and wash away);
- use non-perfumed soap, never applying it inside the vulva;
- wash hair after the bath so your daughter will not be sitting in soapy water for too long;
- make sure your daughter wipes herself properly after bowel movements, that is, thoroughly front to back, without wiping forward again with the same piece of toilet paper;
- wash underwear with gentle soap and rinse several times to eliminate all trace of detergent;
- buy your daughter loose underwear, pale-coloured and cotton;
- make sure your daughter's vulva is kept dry; it should be pat dry after bathing, without rubbing at the skin;
- finally, if necessary, apply zinc-based cream to the irritated area.

If symptoms persist, do not hesitate to contact your doctor.

▶ **My little girl has vaginal discharge. What should I do?**

Before puberty, vaginal discharge can sometimes indicate infection, especially if discharge is abundant. In this case, it will be accompanied by redness of the vulva, and is referred to as "vulvovaginitis." In case of major irritation, girls may also complain of burning when they urinate.

It can help to have the child sit in the tub for ten minutes or so, in plain water, without soap or any other products. If redness and discharge continue, or recur frequently, or if the child has recently suffered a sore throat or fever, it is best to consult your family doctor.

▸ What physical changes are associated with puberty?

The term "puberty" refers to a stage of biological maturation in which girls and boys pass from the physiological status of children to that of adults, and become capable of procreation. On an average, puberty begins at 10 or 11 for girls and 11 or 12 for boys. These changes are caused by hormones, whose production is triggered by the brain. Hormones enter the bloodstream and travel to different parts of the body, causing the changes that make boys and girls become fertile. For girls, the principal hormone is oestrogen; the male hormone is testosterone.

There are several physical indicators that puberty has begun. For girls, these are breast development and the growth of hair in the genital region and underarms, as well as the activation of sweat glands in the genital and underarm regions. The ovaries, vagina and uterus develop; the clitoris and vaginal lips grow bigger. This is also the time when most young girls start to menstruate. The average age for the onset of menstruation is about 12-and-a half, though a young woman's periods can also start a couple of years before or after that age. With the arrival of periods and the rituals of hygiene that become necessary, the young woman develops a new relationship with her body. The vaginal region becomes more lubricated, especially in the presence of sexual excitement. This sensation can make young girls feel uncomfortable at first. If this is the case for your daughter, explain that the vagina is a humid zone and mucous membrane, similar to the mouth, and that there is nothing unclean about it, on the contrary.

As for boys, hair appears in the genital area and armpits, and on the face. The penis and scrotum increase in size and the shoulders grow wider. The boy will have far more frequent erections and sooner or later, will experience ejaculation, which often happens during sleep. It is important to talk to boys about these physical manifestations so they will not feel ashamed or disgusted by them.

▶ When should we talk to girls about menstruation?

Around the age of 7 or 8, it is important to talk to girls about menstruation, answer their questions and reassure them if they are afraid. You can explain that after a certain age, girls' bodies start to prepare each month to make a baby. One can also specify that the foetus develops inside the uterus and that when there is no baby, the protective envelope (sac) in which the baby would have developed, leaves the body through bleeding. It is important to emphasize that this is a natural phenomenon, and that what comes out of the body is not "unclean"; also that sanitary napkins or tampons are used to absorb the blood. One can mention that some girls experience unpleasant sensations, without going so far as to say that some also have terrible cramps! That subject may be saved for a later time, if it is relevant.

Sex-related behaviour

▶ How should we react when our child masturbates?

Masturbation makes some adults uncomfortable. They see it as a bad habit, wondering if it is normal and what limits should be imposed. In fact, it is a normal and frequent behaviour even for young children. An overly restrictive or punitive attitude on the part of parents can lead children to give up their masturbatory activities but also develop feelings of guilt about sexual pleasure. Children can decide to bypass parental restrictions and continue in secret, but this is likely to cause inner conflict. Parents who strictly forbid their children to touch their genitals can cause a disturbance in children's sexual development. Then there are parents who hesitate to define a place and time for this behaviour, or talk about it too much. They do this so their children will be sexually well adjusted, guilt-free, and possess a good knowledge of their bodies. However, the children of such parents might experience these attitudes as an invasion of their privacy or an encouragement to increase this activity, which can lead to sexual over-stimulation.

Later, around the age of 5 or 6, children are generally more discreet about masturbation because they have acquired the notion of privacy. Once parents have explained to children that they can go to their rooms, we expect that the parents will respect children's privacy and not tiptoe up to their bedroom door. On the other hand, if children go away by themselves too often to masturbate, they should be drawn out of their isolation and encouraged to do something more constructive. Compulsive masturbation often causes more of the anxiety that it is meant to appease. Finding the source of children's anxiety and trying to get them interested in other activities will help them move on.

The best thing to do if you walk in on your child masturbating in a non-private space (in the living room, for example) is to explain that there are more appropriate places for them to do what they are doing, that it is an unnecessary activity, and most of all one that should be done privately.

▸ Are my child's sexual games normal? If not, what should I do?

It is sometimes difficult to know if a sexualized game or behaviour is normal. Should we set boundaries, provide information or simply let children play their games in peace?

Generally speaking, sexual play and exploration arise as a natural part of role games, such as playing doctor or playing house. In all cases, the sexual components of games are neither isolated nor particularly planned. Roles assigned to playmates can vary, for example, a little boy can play Mommy. Sexual games can be played between children of the same gender without this being an indicator of their future sexual orientation. In these games between children, there is often an initiator, not always the same child; the situation is not abusive if the initiating child does not exercise undue influence over the others, and is capable of empathy and good judgment.

> ▶ **What attitudes should we adopt with children who behave in a sexually inappropriate manner?**

It can sometimes happen that sexual games are played too frequently, become too important to children or take disturbing turns. As much as sexual games contribute to the discovery of self and others, they can also lead to the abuse of power of one child over another. We have cause to worry if we discover children expressing anger, sadness or aggressiveness over the course of a sexual game. We must ask ourselves what is really going on, and intervene more firmly or consult a professional.

To remember

Parents do not have to feel unduly worried about these sexual games as long as the games are compatible with children's stage of development, are only occasional and not played with overly-intense or negative emotion. If this is the case, we can feel reassured and let children play with minimal intervention.

Attitudes to adopt with children displaying troubling sexual behaviour

Be vigilant

· Do not leave children who display problematic sexual behaviour with others of the same age or younger. Parents must be vigilant. The message you will be conveying is this: "You have trouble controlling yourself? Well, I'm going to help you do it."

· Do not allow children who display problematic sexual behaviour to go to the bathroom with another child or play with others behind closed doors.

· Do not leave them alone for too long.

· When children are "caught in the act", intervene calmly, warmly but firmly, making it clear what is permitted and what is not. Explain that it is the behaviour that is "not good," not the children themselves, and that you are willing to help them.

Communicate to children notions of privacy and respect

· Discuss modesty and privacy with children, and apply these principles in your relationships with them. For example, the bathroom and bedroom are private places whose doors may be closed and where everyone must knock before entering.

· Interrupt sexual jokes or stories, and set an example as an adult.

Inform and support at an emotional level

· Respond to children's concerns about sex, giving them clear and coherent information.

· Tell children that you are available if they want to talk; answer their questions and generally take care of them.

Help children find ways of putting a stop to worrying behaviour

· Help children find recreational activities and appropriate physical games so they can experience pleasures shared with peers or family members.

Did you know?

With the onset of menstruation, a girl's fertility becomes fact. An aspect of her body's inner life has become visible. Menstruation is a concrete indicator of the passage to womanhood. The development of a boy's manhood has no indicator that is quite so clear.

Communication

▸ **When and how should we talk to our child about sex?**

Talking to children about sex does not mean exposing them to sex as it is understood or experienced by adults. Parents must put themselves in the children's place, and try to imagine what they see and understand. A poorly adapted piece of information does not help children grow. At best, it is useless, at worst (and unfortunately, this is what happens all too often), it frightens them and assaults their imagination.

Children must learn about sex early, and the information must be authentic. It is often necessary, though difficult, to strike a "happy medium" between saying too much and not enough. However, it is important to always tell the truth, avoiding myths about babies conceived by magic or penises that fall off because they are touched too often.

Did you know?

Sexuality plays a fundamental role in the psychic development of handicapped children but because of their physical or intellectual limitations, their psychosexual development follows a course of its own. Still, like all children, handicapped children must be allowed to express themselves in the search for pleasure and identity.

Moreover, it is preferable to use the correct terms to designate the parts of the body, including the genitals. For some people these words remain taboo. They resort to words like "wee-wee" or "tee-tee" to avoid saying penis and vagina. The correct words for genital organs will serve children for life, so why not start by using them now, especially since children understand and learn them just as easily as they do other new words?

▶ **My five-year-old never asks about sex. What should we do?**

Daily life provides numerous opportunities for broaching the subject of sex with children. The changing of little sister's diapers or the bath shared between brother and sister are times when anatomical difference is noticed and can be discussed. A kiss exchanged by Mommy and Daddy or a couple on television can introduce the topic of the special relationship between people who love each other, even if they are the same sex – a fact that astonishes some children. Undressing and rituals of hygiene provide other opportunities to discuss privacy, the respect of one's own body and the bodies of others.

Some answers to children's questions

▶ **What does it mean to "make love" ?**
What are "sexual relations"?

Making love and having sex are similar, you can explain. Both expressions refer to two people exchanging special hugs, kisses and caresses, pleasant to give and to receive. This kind of touching and cuddling is for adults who like each other very much; only parents and lovers can do these things.

If children ask for the details of these "special caresses", you can reply that the lovers are cuddled together and touch each other all over their bodies. You may specify that this activity is pleasant for both, but that it is for adults only.

▶ **How are babies made?**

Sooner or later, all children want to know where babies come from. They must be given information that is simple, reliable and concise. For a baby to be made, there needs to be a daddy and a mommy. The daddy gives a little seed that meets a little egg in the mommy's stomach. Together the seed and egg become a baby that slowly grows in the mother's stomach, in a place called the uterus that protects the foetus, keeps it warm and fed for nine months until the baby is ready to come out.

▶ How do Daddy's seed and Mommy's egg meet inside her stomach?

Children who are a little older often ask this question. It is important to tell them how it really happens, remembering that it is all part of a natural process. Children understand that fertilization occurs during sex. The father's penis enters the mother's vagina. Later, it can be explained that the seed is contained in a liquid that comes out of the father's penis. This liquid allows the seed to make its way to the egg in the mother's stomach, or more precisely, her uterus. School-aged children, who require more scientific explanations, can be told about the spermatozoa and the ovum. Pre-teens should be told about contraception.

It is important to tell boys that though they do not yet have seeds (or sperm) that come out of their penis, they will when they are older. Girls can be told that if they want, they can have babies when they are older.

▶ How and where do babies come out?

You may say, "Remember that to make a baby, the daddy has to put his penis in the mommy's vagina, to leave his sperm. When the baby is ready to be born, it leaves the mother's stomach and comes out of the vagina, which is made for that purpose. In a way, the vagina is both the entrance and the exit for the baby."

▶ Why do women have breasts?

As a matter of fact, both women and men have breasts. Little girls' breasts will grow bigger, unlike those of little boys. When a woman has a baby, her breasts naturally produce milk to feed her baby.

▸ **Will my penis grow?**

A boy sometimes wonders if his penis will remain small for his whole life. You may tell him that since he was born, all parts of his body have grown, including his penis, and his whole body will keep growing until full puberty, when he has become a big teenage boy. You might also add that not all boys grow at the same pace, that all boys' legs and feet are not the same size, and that the same goes for the penis.

▸ **Why does my penis get bigger?**

"There are a few reasons that your penis gets bigger. Sometimes it gets bigger when you really have to pee. Sometimes it gets bigger when you touch it and you get a nice tingling feeling. It is normal, it happens to all little boys, and is called "having an erection."

Education and prevention

▶ **How should we react to the excessive representation of sex in advertising and other media?**

Children are bombarded with images and information from the media. The media often provides a distorted image of love, sex, and the relations between men and women. The sex act is trivialized and pleasure depicted as instant gratification. Parental vigilance is advised. Not necessarily to censor or control what young people see and hear, but to make sure they are not left to interpret media messages alone. Make sure they have access to reliable people with whom they can talk about what they see. In order to be credible in your supervision and guidance, it is important to be familiar with what interests your children. Watch the latest music videos with them, ask their opinion of the clothes a lead singer or movie star is wearing; go shopping with children and negotiate. This creates opportunities to discuss what we find acceptable or unacceptable; having "done your homework," for example by watching music videos with your child, your arguments will be more valid. In this way too, you may avoid being overly strict, and arrive at certain compromises with children: "This piece of clothing is not for school, but you can wear it on weekends."

Children must be taught to analyse and be critical about media messages. Discuss hidden issues in advertising, such as how companies make profits thanks to young people without any concern for how their advertising affects them.

Remember that television and the Internet are not legitimate resources for sex education because they do not necessarily answer young people's questions or calm their anxieties. On the other hand, they can serve as accessories, as long as parents supervise and interpret, and offer guidance to children who spend long hours exposed to these media.

Finally, do not be afraid to take a firm stand about your convictions. Ultimately, it is up to adults to make certain decisions, even though it means your young person will sometimes have to put up with a little frustration.

▶ How can I protect my child from sexual abuse?

Children have neither the necessary experience nor the maturity to recognize when people want to take advantage of them, abuse and hurt them. This prospect is a great source of worry for parents. How do we protect children from such harmful and traumatic experiences? How do we teach children to interact with their environment without overly emphasizing the fact that they are vulnerable just because they are children? How do we do this without frightening them for no good reason?

Prevention programmes for children (such as "street-proofing") approach such questions in a variety of ways. Generally, children are told that their bodies belong to them and that they are allowed to refuse if someone wants to touch them, stroke their genitals or any other part of them. They are guided towards an understanding of the differences between "good" and "bad" touching, and to recognize situations of danger. In these programmes, they discuss the idea of "secrets:" there are secrets that we enjoy keeping to ourselves, and others that make us sad - those are the ones that it is important to reveal. Children are also guided to identify trustworthy people they can talk to and accept help from. The ultimate goal is to make children less vulnerable, without at the same time leading them to suspect everyone around them.

It is generally considered that these programmes make children more competent, allowing some to reveal sexual abuse of which they have been victim. But it is essential to consider a child's age when it comes to prevention; it is a matter of efficiency and respect for the child. We must not forget that children, especially very young ones, do not understand certain messages, which may seem very obvious to us. Moreover, giving children pieces of information here and there is not an effective solution; though it may be useful to provide them with certain facts, other kinds of information could upset their peace of mind.

Children need to hear about love, first and foremost, much more than they need to hear about the risks of assault. This is the heart of prevention. To learn to know oneself, take care of oneself, have self-esteem, self-respect, and trust for oneself, to be able to express emotions and communicate with others, these are the cornerstones of prevention. Prevention should complement a child's general sexual education. Talking to children about physical and emotional privacy teaches them to consider their body and sexuality as something precious and worthy of respect. They feel more relaxed about their sexuality, more ready to take a stand if anyone makes them propositions, and defend themselves if necessary.

However, in spite of all our efforts at prevention and information, children remain vulnerable. They remain at a disadvantage in relation to adults or older children who have power and influence over them. We cannot ask children to take charge of their own safety. The prevention of sexual abuse is certainly not their responsibility, but that of the adults who want to protect them. We owe it to children to guarantee the competence of the people to whom we entrust their care, ensure children's safety in the streets (for example, that they are accompanied to school), make sure we know all the people they come in contact with, and be aware of who they are with at a given moment.

Appendix
normal psychosexual development in children from 0 to 12 years

Children from 1 to 2 years

- In their close relationship with their parents, children experience sensual contact all over their bodies.

- Little by little, children psychically grow away from the figure of the mother (separation-individuation process) and can become attached to a favourite object (transitional object) symbolizing the mother when she is not there.

- From 0 to 15 months, the mouth is an important erogenous zone through which children explore the world and experience pleasure (oral stage).

- From 15 months to 2 ½ years, the anal zone becomes important in terms of sensation and various developmental issues (anal stage, the learning of sphincter control as well as control of self and relations with others).

- Children thoroughly explore their bodies, driven by curiosity and the quest for sensual pleasure.

- The reflex reactions of erection and lubrication occur. Rather than reactions to erotic stimulation, these are responses to touch (for example, during diaper changes), to friction or the need to urinate.

- Boys discover their genitals at around 8 months and girls at around 10-12 months, with occasional genital autostimulation.
- From the age of 20 months, masturbation is frequent. Its objective is to achieve a calming effect (sometimes through a rocking movement), comfort and pleasure.
- Children like to be naked and look at or touch other people's bodies.
- Children are curious about elimination and increasingly interested in male-female anatomical differences.
- This is the beginning of gender identity; children can distinguish between girls and boys through external attributes like clothing and hairstyle.
- With language acquisition, the child can name the parts of the body, including the genitals.

Children from 3 to 5 years

- This is the time of concrete thinking and magical thinking, of imagination, of a variety of fantasies and fears. Children gradually make a clearer distinction between real and imaginary.
- Symbolization has been achieved and children often play role-playing games (house, doctor...), driven by curiosity and the desire to try out different sex roles.
- There is increased attachment and desire to be close to the opposite sex parent (Oedipal phase).

- In this context, children assert their own gender; the formation of sexual identity is in progress.
- Children display a marked interest in anatomical difference, where babies come from, elimination and body orifices.
- Children masturbate occasionally, motivated by the need for relaxation, comfort or pleasure.
- Increased exhibitionism (children like to be naked and to show themselves off) and voyeurism (they are interested in other people's bodies, both adults and children) at bath time, during rituals of grooming and hygiene, or while getting dressed.
- Children want to touch parts of their parents' bodies (breasts, penis), their motivation having to do with curiosity and limit-seeking rather than sex.
- They occasionally play sexual games with friends or brothers and sisters (mutual exploration).
- They refer verbally to elimination and sexual anatomy (peepee, poop, bum, fart!).

Children from 6 to 8 years (latency)

- On one hand, children enter the world of school; they feel the desire to conform to social norms, they assimilate the knowledge of what is done and not done (e.g. increased privacy about sex) and social conventions pertaining to sex and sex roles.
- On the other hand, children need privacy and are physically modest in the family sphere; they are embarrassed by nudity and references to sex.

- They express disgust towards heterosexual relations and choose to keep company with their peers of the same sex.

- There is a return to better relations with the same-sex parent (resolution of the "Oedipal complex").

- They also display occasional lapses of inhibition (a lapse of defense mechanisms), occasional private masturbation, secret sexual games with their peers (body comparisons, mutual touching). These games may be played with the same or the opposite sex without being indicators of future sexual orientation.

- They exchange information with peers and ask adults more precise questions about conception and birth; the development of abstract thinking contributes to these new lines of questioning.

- They make jokes and sometimes use vulgar language, the meaning of which they do not really understand.

- Their sense of sexual identity is established and remains constant.

- Social role-playing is important.

Children (pre-teen) from 9 to 12 years

- During this period of transition towards adolescence, there is the onset of puberty and the development of secondary sexual characteristics, which gives rise to a sense of pride or self-consciousness.

- The development of self-image is strongly affected by the comments of others and comparisons with the norm (assimilation of social norms).
- Pre-teens experience sexual sensations and private, or sometimes mutual masturbation (at this stage, more clearly motivated by the quest for orgasmic pleasure).
- They begin to have fantasies with sexual connotations.
- The interest in the opposite sex increases; boys and girls start going out together and experience physical intimacy (kisses, mutual fondling).
- Pre-teens seek information on the functioning of sex organs and talk about it with their peers.
- Pre-teens display physical modesty and express the need for privacy about nudity.
- Pre-teens have an increased awareness of their identity and sexual orientation.

To learn more about child's sexuality

RICHARDSON, Justin and Mark A. SCHUSTER. *Everything You Never Wanted Your Kids To Know About Sex, But Were Afraid They'd Ask: The secrets to surviving your child's sexual development from birth to the teens.* New York: Crown Publishers, 2003. 388 p.

HAFFNER, Debra W. *From Diapers to Dating: A parent's guide to raising sexually healthy children.* New York: Newmarket Press, 1999. 224 p.

BERKENKAMP, Lauri and Steven C. ATKINS. *Talking To Your Kids About Sex: From toddlers to preteens.* Norwich, VT.: Nomad Press, 2002. 127 p.

MAXWELL, Sharon. *The Talk : What Your Kids Need to Hear from You about Sex.* New York: Avery, 2008. 219 p.

IN THE SAME COLLECTION

What Should I Know about my Child's Self-Esteem ?
Germain Duclos

What Should I Know about my Teen?
Céline Boisvert

My Child's Development
Francine Ferland

Mixed Sources
Product group from well-managed forests,
controlled sources and recycled wood or fiber
www.fsc.org   Cert no. SGS-COC-003885
© 1996 Forest Stewardship Council

Printed in Quebec
by Litho Chic inc.
on May 2009